The Bettyad, a Poem: descriptive of the progress of the Young Roscius in London.

George Moutard Woodward

THE

BETTYAD,

A POEM.

PRICE TWO SHILLINGS AND SIXPENCE.

STRIKING LIKENESSES OF John Bull AND THE Young Roscius.

Pub.d by M. Allen 15 Paternoster Row Jan.y 10. 1805.

THE
BETTYAD,

A POEM:

DESCRIPTIVE OF THE PROGRESS

OF THE

YOUNG ROSCIUS

IN

LONDON.

BY

G. M. WOODWARD,

Author of ECCENTRIC EXCURSIONS THROUGH ENGLAND AND WALES, &c.

John Bull—John Bull—thy ears ſtretch wide,
Thy wig ſet ſtraight—whate'er betide,
   The Bard the news ſhall tell:
To gain the truth he has contriv'd,
Know, Maſter BETTY's juſt arriv'd
   At RICHARDSON's Hotel!

Vide POEM.

LONDON:

PRINTED AND PUBLISHED BY M. ALLEN, 15, PATERNOSTER-ROW.

1805.

THE

BETTYAD.

WHAT founds confus'd falute my ears?
From Priefts, from Poets, Actors, Peers!
   What Mania fills the town?
Smiles, greetings, falutations, all
One buz of joy 'mongft great and fmall,
   The world's fure upfide down!

Oh! blefh ma heart—old Levi cries,
Dear me!—the Chriftian Mifs replies;
   Ben Block, too, aids the clatter:
Huzzas augment the fwelling tide,
Pleafure prevails on ev'ry fide,
   JOHN BULL cries, What's the matter?

The matter, JOHN! thy ears ſtretch wide,
Thy wig ſet ſtraight, whate'er betide,
 The Bard the news ſhall tell:
To gain the truth, he has contriv'd,
Know, Maſter BETTY's juſt arriv'd
 At RICHARDSON's Hotel!!

As ſwift as light the tidings flew,
And thouſands to the manſion drew,
 Deficient of employ:
Their mouths they open'd with ſurpriſe,
And like to ſaucers ſtretch'd their eyes,
 In hope to ſee the Boy.

But he, by travel ſomewhat jaded,
Towards his chamber ſlow paraded,
 As if by inſtinct led:
Yet though he felt in weary plight,
He wiſh'd Papa and Ma good night,
 And then went up to bed!

Though trifles light as thefe appear
Too tedious for a critic's ear,
   Still muft the Mufe relate,
All that to Roscius appertains,
More than her common routine ftrains,
   Or e'en affairs of ftate!

Next morn, as foon as he arofe,
After a fweet and found repofe,
   And breakfaft ate in hurry,
He took at fkipping-rope a hop,
Play'd dumps—and fpun his *humming-top*,
   Then call'd on Mr. Mu———y!

John K—ble long before that time,
In cogitation quite fublime,
   Sat mufing on the theme;
But as to drawing all before him,
And gaining millions to adore him,
   John thought it all a dream!

B

Around each houfe a murmur ran,
And feiz'd on woman, child, and man,
 Poor Slo——r look'd quite blue;
And Mrs. Rei——e, for dreffes fam'd,
And Dib——n, low in pulfe exclaim'd,
 Our Pantomimes won't do!

At night our Hero faw the play,
In brown great coat, fome people fay,
 Though others fay 'twas blue;
But which the Mufe will not pretend
Her fanction either fide to lend,
 Though this fhe'll vouch as true,

A belcher round his neck he wore,
Which fome pronounc'd was quite a bore,
 Still all could not conceal him;
John Bull his little favourite fpied,
And foon as he his features eyed,
 With fhouts aloud reveal'd him!

Alarm'd, no doubt, at fuch a noife,
Which might have frightened elder boys,
   His eyes around him fkimming,
He fought the door, and made a dart,
Well pleas'd with lobby beaux to part,
   And all the naughty women!

In private box, he got a nook,
And liften'd ferioufly to C——k,
   In Richard's part fublime;
And then—no wonder great I ween,
Like other boys about thirteen,
   Admired the Pantomime.

Some fay that firft to Drury's pile,
He went the hours to beguile,
   Prince Hamlet was the play:
But whether ELL——N's gay eafe,
Or other matters fail'd to pleafe,
   He fhortly came away.

But now, O Muse, awhile take breath,
Prepare for squeezing near to death,
  The sun peeps out quite pretty:
The day arrives, the country's boast,
Great Barbarossa rules the roast,
  And Achmet—Master BETTY!

The Peer forgets his high descent,
On ROSCIUS, and his fame full bent,
  And Peeresses the same;
The Cit right westward bends his way,
Once more to see a London play,
  All arm in arm, with dame.

The Tailor quits his threads and sheers,
Ben Bowsprit also that way steers,
  With pretty Sue in tow:
The Barber leaves his soap and suds,
And Grooms and Jockies fav'rite studs,
  Resolv'd to see the show!

By three o'clock the crowds arrive,
And anxious wait till half paſt five,
   As merry as young grigs:
The door unbarr'd—his fate each rues,
Some loſe their hats, and ſome their ſhoes,
   And ladies loſe their wigs!

Then ſome get in, and ſome ſtay out,
Some giggle pleas'd, while others pout,
   Some mourn their broken ſtitches;
While Ladies, Beaux from depth of pit
To boxes raiſe in fainting fit,
   By waiſtband of their breeches!

STOR—CE, BRA—M, and the reſt,
With Miſs DE CA—P, in order plac'd,
   Were very early twiddlers;
While INC———N, with modeſt grace,
Reſolv'd to get the *foremast* place,
   Sat ſnug amongſt the Fiddlers*.

* The Gentlemen of the Orchestra, Musical Composers, &c. will excuse the Author, for making use of the word *Fiddlers*, when he

C   assures

And now CHA—S KEM—LE, with a face

As long as wideſt ſheers embrace,

   March'd forward to addreſs,

While TAY—R, author of the ſame,

Try'd to keep up his drooping frame,

   He ſure could do no leſs.

But ſuch a noiſe their Godſhips led,

Thinking the little boy was dead,

   It made Olympus roar!

So finding all his efforts vain,

He modeſtly march'd back again,

   And word ſpake never more!

Still noiſe and riot grate the ear,

But lo!—YOUNG ROSCIUS now draws near,

   JOHN BULL, entranc'd, cries huſh!

assures them he did so merely to rhyme with the word *Twiddlers*, without the most remote allusion to their twiddling or fiddling immense sums from the pockets of JOHN BULL.

'Tis filence all—what grace and air,
And then his bow, fo debonair,
   Makes Dancing Mafters blufh!

Each look, each action fpeaks, and tells
The varied notes, the thrilling fwells,
   A fecond GARRICK plays!!
The curtain drops, and honeft JOHN,
To crown the whole, bench gets upon,
   And gives three loud huzzas!!

Great P—T, and Lordly MELV—E, hight
Procured places fnug that night,
   And as fome people fay,
The firft, and only time, no doubt,
To fhun the noify rabble rout,
   Got in a private way!

Next day, the Sunday prints fo grave,
All other fubjects careful wave,
   From Critic's lafh to free him;

Recorder—Meſſenger—Review,
All give Young BETTY honours due;
  Th' OBSERVER *did not see him!**

Then comes the Chronicle, and Poſt,
The Herald, Times, and all the hoſt
  Prepare their inquiſition:
Their critic ink begins to flow,
And Printers' Devils in a row
  Are put in requiſition!

Still incenſe all to BETTY raiſe,
E'en wand'ring Syrens chaunt his praiſe,
  And hail the wond'rous creature:
In ev'ry corner Portraits ſtrike,
And ſtrange to ſay, not two alike,
  Yet all pourtray'd from Nature!

* This *discerning* print began his Critique on the performance in
nearly the above words.

Lives!—Medals!—Anecdotes! invite,

To tempt the monied curious wight,

   Gay—witty—grave—explicit:

Card invitations quickly fly,

Princes and Peers all anxious try

   To gain th' earlieſt viſit!

A rival BETTY too lays claim

To ſome few grains of public fame,

   Well known throughout the land:

He hopes you'll viſit on the days

His little name-ſake BETTY plays,

   His Chop-houſe in the Strand!*

Next Douglas greets th' anxious rows,

And Frederick charms the Belles and Beaux,

   Till call'd to Drury Lane:

---

* A Chop-House known many years under the name of BETTY's,
facing the New Church, in the Strand.

There Norval ftill his vot'ries draws,
And fhouts, and loud unmix'd applaufe,
   Re-echo through the fane!

Glenalvon, play'd by BAR——E,
Prepares his rival to explore,
   Enough one's blood to harrow:
So have I feen with leering eye,
Grimalkin from a wall on high,
   Obferve a young cock-fparrow!

One night a play, by high command,
Concluded:——SHE—Y took his ftand,
   With BETTY, Fame's foreftaller;
The K——, God blefs him, look'd that way,
And thus, afide, was heard to fay,
   " I thought the Boy was taller!"

Thus daily rifing in renown,
The charm, the idol of the town!
   The praife of young and old:

How painful then the Mufe's tafk,
To tell—Oh what? the world will afk,
  Young BETTY took a cold!!

But WRO———N, in a plaintive ſtrain,
Declar'd he ſhould not play again
| Till holidays were over;
And more, to do all pain away,
Declar'd that till that happy day,
  The Boy ſhould live in clover.

Thus ends the Mufe her frolic play,
But ſhould a Bard in *serious* lay,
  Attack his juſt renown;
Or on pale Envy's tablet write
A line his well-earn'd praiſe to blight,
  Her hand ſhall tear it down.

F I N I S.